# English for Au Pairs

## The Au Pair's guide to learning English

# English for Au Pairs

## The Au Pair's guide to learning English

by Lucy Curtis

illustrated by Lucy Letherland

MARION BOYARS

London • New York

Published in the United Kingdom in 2013 by

Marion Boyars Publishers
26 Parke Road
London
SW13 9NG

www.marionboyars.co.uk

1 2 3 4 5 6 7 8 9 10
© Lucy Curtis, 2013

Original paperback ISBN: 978-0-7145-3156-4

A British Library Cataloguing in Publication record for this book is available
from the British Library.

Designed and typeset by Lucy Letherland in 9.5 on 13 pt Helvetica Neue

Printed by Latimer Trend, Plymouth, UK

# Introduction

**by Catheryn Kilgarriff, Publisher**

Every year, thousands of young women, and some young men, leave their countries and arrive in England to look after children, live with a family, and learn English. The host families have to adjust to a person from a different country, and there are a multitude of differences and misunderstandings, on both sides.

I had the idea for this book when a new young woman came to clean our house. She is called Marta, and she comes from Poland.

I asked Marta what her background was, and she told me that she had recently graduated with a degree in journalism from a university in Poland. A break up from a boyfriend had spurred her to make this huge change in her life, and she had arrived in London with a friend, and they were both cleaners, sharing a room.

Marta's English was good, but I soon noticed that it did not progress. In fact, some weeks, it seemed to have gone backwards, and soon she started using phrases like "Hello, darlin'," just like an old fashioned char-lady.

I thought - what if she could learn English properly? What makes her so different from our au pairs, when our children were younger? A lot of our au pairs found English hard, and some did not pass their exams. When I looked at the text books they were using, I could see why they did not like the lessons.

I knew that English for Cleaners was unlikely to take off, so my thoughts returned to au pairs. I still think that most of their text books, although grammatically useful, have content that is a million miles away from their day to day experience of being in a new household. I also thought that the host families may not know how to handle the many situations which crop up, and that they would appreciate a book which included them as characters.

So, I decided to commission a book from Lucy Curtis, who also has employed au pairs, as well as run a language school teaching them English. She also had jobs as an au pair, while she was studying Modern Languages at Oxford University. I wanted a book which was relevant to the au pairs, and one that would make them laugh. I hope that prospective host families will read it, and find it fun, and use it to help the young people learn English.

# Contents

**Appendices**

*To my family*
*... and all the au pairs I've*
*had the pleasure of knowing.*

**Lucy Curtis**

# 1. Now I am a member of an English family

My head is in an oven. What am I doing here? The oven is very dirty and I am cleaning it. My host mother wants me to clean this dirty oven and also the fridge. It is my first day as an au pair.

I am Marta and I arrived last night at 9pm after a long journey from my home in Poland. My host mother collected me from the airport. She was in a hurry and she said very little in the car.

The children were in bed when I arrived here last night. Now they are on their way to school. I don't know this family and I don't know my way around this house. No one is here and I feel alone.

It is now 9 o' clock in the morning and my new life is beginning. I must clean the oven and the fridge. After that, there are more jobs. There is a list on the table. It says:

- *load the dishwasher*
- *hang out the washing*
- *wash the kitchen floor*
- *bleach the toilets*
- *clean the bathrooms*
- *do the ironing*
- *dust the furniture*
- *vacuum all the carpets*

My host mother is taking the children to school. My host father works in London. I am still very tired after my long journey here last night. I woke up at 8.30am this morning and there was a note for me from my host mother. It says: *We usually get up at 7.15am. I am taking the children to school - back at 1pm. Here's a list of jobs to do this morning.*

I am very hungry, so I'm looking for something to eat for breakfast. In the fridge there is a pot of yoghurt. It's delicious!

\* \* \* \* \* \* \*

It is 1.15pm and my host mother is back. She is not happy with me because I ate her yoghurt. It is her special yoghurt and I must not eat it. She is also angry because the oven is not clean enough. I feel uncomfortable.

It is 3pm and I am still ironing. My host mother is asking me to make a Shepherd's Pie for tea. I do not know what Shepherd's Pie is. Now she looks angry again and I feel unhappy.

I am in my room and I am phoning the au pair agency. The lady at the agency is kind. I feel upset because the host mother wants me to do heavy-duty cleaning, but my job is to do light housework only. I explain that my host mother doesn't treat me like a member of the family and they do not want me to eat their food!

The lady at the agency understands my problem. She asks me, "Do you want to move to another family?" I am trying not to cry as I say, "Yes, please." The agency is looking for another family for me. I feel so glad!

# Useful tips

Use an agency to find your host family. That way, if there is a problem and you need to change families, the agency will be able to help you. The British Au Pair Agencies Association has a list of approved agencies. See **www.bapaa.org.uk** or **www.IAPA.org** for further details.

Before you start, make sure you and your host family both agree how many hours you will work each day and what your responsibilities are.

# Brush up on your English ...

### Present continuous
Use the present continuous for things which are happening now, at the moment of speaking.
e.g. My host mother is taking the children to school.

*Positive form*
She is taking the children to school.
*Negative form*
She isn't (is not) taking the children to school.
*Question form*
Is she taking the children to school?
*Negative question form*
Isn't she taking the children to school?

### Present simple
Use the present simple for habitual truths.
e.g. My host father works in London.

*Positive form*
He works in London.
*Negative form*
He doesn't (does not) work in London.
*Question form*
Does he work in London?

*Negative question form*
Doesn't he work in London?

Some verbs never or rarely take the continuous form. These are verbs which describe states as opposed to actions. State verbs relate to:

*mental and emotional states* - love, hate, prefer, think, understand, remember, feel, know, believe, suppose.
*senses* - see, smell, hear, taste, feel.
*communications and causing reactions* - look (seem), agree, disagree, deny, mean, promise, surprise, satisfy, astonish, impress, please.
*possession and other verbs* - be, belong, need, have, contain, fit, include, measure, owe, own, possess, want, weigh.

## Have a go!

**1A.** Choose the correct verb form

**1.** We usually are having / have breakfast at 7.30am.

**2.** What time do you wake up / are you waking up each morning?

**3.** My host father works / is working every day in London.

**4.** The oven doesn't smell / isn't smelling nice.

**5.** Are you liking / do you like yoghurt?

**6.** At the moment I am doing / I do the ironing.

**7.** My host mother doesn't understand me / isn't understanding me.

**8.** It is 3pm and I am still ironing / still iron.

**9.** The children go / are going to school every day.

**10.** I don't know / am not knowing how to cook Shepherd's Pie.

**See p.82 for answers**

# 2. I can't speak English! Help!

"Where's my school bag?" asked Eliza.
"I can't brush my hair!" cried Daisy.
"Does anyone know where my football boots are?" yelled Charlie.
"Get in the car, we're late!" shouted my new host mother.
"Bye, Marta!" they called as they all left the house.

I changed families yesterday. I was working with my first family for two days before the agency found a new one for me. I have been staying in the UK for less than a week and I have already changed families!

Now I live in Mayford, a small town outside London. There are three children - Eliza, aged 9, Charlie aged 7, Daisy aged 3 and my host mum will have another baby in a few months! Everything is going

well, so far. My first job of the day is to help get the children ready for school. I must also clear away the breakfast things and load the dishwasher.

Eliza and Charlie go to a primary school and Daisy goes to a nursery three mornings each week. Daisy is lovely. When she is not at nursery I play with her. When she is at nursery

I tidy the children's bedrooms and I do the ironing. In the evenings I help get the children ready for bed. This is not too difficult - it's light housework and I like working with the children.

* * * * * * *

I have been spending a lot of time on my computer talking to my friends and family at home in Poland. I miss my friends. Sometimes it is lonely being an au pair, especially when everyone is talking about something and I don't understand. I am impatient to start my English classes so I can meet some other au pairs here.

Last night, I was reading in my room when my host mum asked me to watch TV with her, so we watched a cookery programme. I was enjoying the programme when suddenly my host mum said, "I feel like a pickled onion." I didn't understand, so I just smiled. Then she asked, "What do you feel like, Marta?" It was a strange question, but I said "I feel normal, thank you." My host mum laughed and said, "What I mean is that I really want to eat a pickled onion! Would you like to eat something too?" So now I have just learnt a new expression. I will write it down!

* * * * * * *

This morning my host mum took me to a college where I can study English. I will have English lessons twice a week. I must pay for the term's classes in advance. I do not have enough money so my host mum will pay half. Cool! The classes will start next week. Next year I hope I can take an exam called First Certificate in English with The University of Cambridge. I know I must study every day. My teacher says I must

read English newspapers, listen to BBC Radio 4, watch television and use a good dictionary in order to improve my English.

I have just received an email from the mother of my first host family. She says she's sorry for being so unfair. She has now separated from her husband and says she has been suffering a lot of stress. Now I understand.

\* \* \* \* \* \* \*

I am still very happy with my new host family. When Eliza and Charlie return from school they are always pleased to see me. Sometimes I help them with their homework. They have tea at

5.30pm and they go to bed at about 7.30pm. Their father, who works in London, comes home from work between 7pm and 8pm, but sometimes he goes away on business trips for a few days.

The children tell me everything about their teachers and their friends at school. Today Eliza said, "Mr Fisher exploded today in our science lesson." I was very surprised to hear this so I asked, "Was he okay?" but Eliza just said "Yeah, he does that sometimes when we're naughty." I want to check the meaning of "to explode" in my dictionary!

This afternoon I went to the public library and became a member. It was very easy. I gave them a letter from the au pair agency to show the address of my host family. Now I can borrow books and films from the library. At the library, I met a French au pair called Céline who is 18, like me! She lives two miles away from me and she has a car. We have been working together all evening to create a page in 'Facebook' called *Mayford Au Pairs*. We hope other au pairs who live near us will find our page and contact us.

\* \* \* \* \* \* \*

I have started my English classes! There are 12 students in the class and nine of us are au pairs. Four of us live in Mayford and the others live nearby. Céline is in the intermediate class, like me. Our teacher is Judith. She has given us some homework. I must complete some grammar exercises and learn a list of irregular verbs. Judith says my understanding is good but I need to improve my colloquial English and my pronunciation.

# Useful tips

Your local county council offers ESOL classes (English for Speakers of Other Languages). You can get information about classes from your nearest public library. Cambridge University offers several different exams which are internationally recognised by employers and universities. See the Cambridge ESOL website **www.cambridgeesol.org** to find out which exam is right for you.

On-line dictionaries and pocket dictionaries can be confusing so it is better to use a large dictionary such as the Dictionary of Contemporary English, published by Longman.

Read newspapers and magazines in order to improve your vocabulary and your colloquial English. Also watch TV and listen to BBC Radio 4 as much as possible. Keep a notebook of new vocabulary and phrases throughout your stay in the UK.

# Brush up on your English ...

### Past simple
Use the past simple for completed actions or states that happened at a particular time in the past.
e.g. I changed families yesterday.

*Positive form*
She changed families yesterday.
*Negative form*
She didn't change families yesterday.
*Question form*
Did she change families yesterday?
*Negative question form*
Didn't she change families yesterday?

## Past continuous

Use the past continuous when something is in progress at a time in the past. This can sometimes be an interrupted action with the next verb in the past simple.

e.g. I was working with my first family for two days before the agency found a new family.

*Positive form*

She was working with her first family for two days before the agency found a new family.

*Negative form*

She wasn't working for her first family for two days before the agency found a new family.

*Questions form*

Was she working for her first family for two days before the agency found a new family?

*Negative question form*

Wasn't she working for her first family for two days before the agency found a new family?

## Present perfect

Use the present perfect to connect the past to the present. The action starts in the past but continues into the present.

e.g. I have started my English classes (and I am continuing them now).

*Positive form*

She has started her English classes.

*Negative form*

She hasn't started her English classes.

*Question form*

Has she started her English classes?

*Negative question form*

Hasn't she started her English classes?

## Present perfect continuous

Use the present perfect continuous for action in the past that was long and repeated or not yet complete.

eg. They have been working together all evening.

*Positive form*
They have been working together all evening.
*Negative form*
They haven't been working together all evening.
*Question form*
Have they been working together all evening?
*Negative question form*
Haven't they been working together all evening?

## Have a go!

**2A.** Find three more examples of the past simple in the text.

1.

2.

3.

**2B.** Find three more examples of the past continuous in the text.

1.

2.

3.

**2C.** Find three more examples of the present perfect in the text.

**1.**

**2.**

**3.**

**2D.** Find three more examples of the present perfect continuous in the text.

**1.**

**2.**

**3.**

See p.82 for answers.

# 3. Getting around

Today I went to my English lesson by train, as usual. I came out of the train station and walked along the pavement towards my school. It is a busy road with lots of traffic and double-decker buses. I reached the zebra crossing and was waiting for the traffic to stop for me, when suddenly there was a lot of noise. I heard people shouting, cars sounding their horns and a bus was flashing its lights. The traffic stopped for me at the zebra crossing and then I saw what was happening. Olga, an au pair from my English class, was travelling along the wrong side of the road, on a pair of roller skates! She waved at me as she went past. She must be mad!

\* \* \* \* \* \* \*

Céline is very lucky. She has a car so she can drive anywhere. She must also drive the children to school and collect them afterwards. Her host family paid for her to do a UK familiarisation driving course so that she is confident about driving here. I don't have to do the school run and I can't use the family car because I'm not allowed to, but that's okay.

I can make Shepherd's Pie! It is really very easy. All you need is some minced lamb, an onion, a carrot, a tin of tomatoes and a few potatoes. You have to cook the chopped onions and carrot and minced meat in a little oil, then add some seasoning such as thyme, salt and pepper, then add the tinned tomatoes and let it cook gently for about 30 minutes. Then you boil some potatoes and mash them with a little butter. Put the meat mixture in an oven dish and spread the mashed potato on top. Add some grated cheese and bake it in the oven for about 30 minutes until it is golden brown on top. Cool!

* * * * * * *

Oh, no! Something terrible has happened to Céline. She parked her car in town this afternoon to do some shopping. When she came back her car was clamped! She parked on two yellow lines

in an area which said NO PARKING. She had to pay £200 to have it released but she didn't have enough money, so it was taken away. Now she has got to pay a fine of £400 to get the car back. Can you believe it? Her host mum must be really upset too.

23

This morning I was doing the ironing in the kitchen when suddenly there was an urgent knock at the back door. It was a lady from the village and she looked very agitated. My host mum asked her in and at that moment, the lady started crying. I decided to put the kettle on to make some tea for her.

The lady told my host mum that her au pair had left that morning without saying good bye and had simply put a letter on the kitchen table to say she was going back to Norway because she missed her boyfriend.

I felt very sorry for her. What a terrible thing to do to your host family! My host mum advised her to tell the agency and let them sort it out.

\* \* \* \* \* \* \*

My host mum has bought a 16-25 Railcard for me. It gives me cheaper train fares. This means I can go to lots of different places by train. Céline and I went on the train today. We went to London to visit some really cool shops in Carnaby Street. At the next station we saw Ricardo get on the train. He's an au pair with a family of boys near Mayford. He's in our class and he can speak English really well. Ricardo was sitting next to us and we were talking together when a ticket inspector arrived. The inspector

said, "Can I see your tickets, please?" I showed him my ticket and my discount card. Céline showed hers also. Suddenly, Ricardo couldn't understand English. I asked him, "Haven't you got a ticket, Ricardo?" but he just looked at me with a peculiar expression. It was very strange! Then the ticket inspector told Ricardo he mustn't get on a train without a ticket.

In the end, Ricardo had to give his full name and address in England. The train company will send him a letter and he will have to pay a fine. Céline was very angry with Ricardo and said he mustn't dodge the train fare again.

# Useful tips

A 16-25 Railcard gives a discount of 33 per cent on train fares for people aged between 16 and 25.

Buy a ticket before you get on the train or you may have to pay a penalty of at least double the actual cost of your ticket.

The Royal Society for the Prevention of Accidents offers driving courses for people driving in the UK for the first time.
See **www.rospa.com** for details.

Do not park on double yellow lines. When you pay for a parking ticket do not exceed your time allowance otherwise your car may be clamped and towed away. It will cost a lot of money to get it back again.

# Brush up on your English ...

## Can / must / have (got) to

### Can
Use 'can' for ability, permission and requests.
e.g. I can make Shepherd's Pie. (I am able)
      I can't use the family car. (not permitted)
      Can I see your tickets, please? (request)

### Must
Use 'must' for necessity or obligation.
e.g. She must drive the children to school.
You can also use 'must' to express a conclusion or explanation.
e.g. Her host mum must be upset!

## Have (got) to

Use 'have to' or 'have got to' when there is an obligation from outside, such as a rule or regulation.

e.g. You've got to show your ticket / you have to show your ticket. (It's the regulation)

## Mustn't / Don't have to

These have different meanings and are not interchangeable.

e.g. You mustn't get on a train without a ticket. (It's prohibited)

I don't have to do the school run. (I am not obliged)

# Have a go!

**3A.** Complete these sentences with the correct form of can, must or have (got) to.

**1.** When the inspector comes you ＿＿＿＿＿ show your ticket.

**2.** ＿＿＿＿＿ I see your tickets, please?

**3.** I don't have permission so I ＿＿＿＿＿ drive my family's car.

**4.** You ＿＿＿＿＿ park on double yellow lines.

**5.** You ＿＿＿＿＿ drive to London, you can get the train instead.

**6.** At 3pm she ＿＿＿＿＿ do the school run.

**7.** Ricardo ＿＿＿＿＿ speak English really well.

**8.** Olga does crazy things, she ＿＿＿＿＿ be mad!

**9.** We don't have any meat or potatoes so we ＿＿＿＿＿ make Shepherd's Pie.

**10.** When your car is clamped you ＿＿＿＿＿ pay a big fine.

**See p.83 for answers.**

# 4. The night club

Mayford is quite a small town. It has some shops, a library, a pizzeria, a couple of cafés and pubs, but there is not much else to do here. I came to England because there are so many things to do here and my home town is very quiet. I am planning to do some really exciting things. My host mum has given me a magazine called Time Out. It has lots of information about entertainment in London such as street markets, cinemas, theatres, art galleries, museums, nightlife and clubs ... I'm going to try and see a musical but the tickets are quite expensive.

* * * * * *

Today, I went with Céline to London to see a musical called The Lion King. It was amazing! We got very cheap tickets the night before for a performance at 2.30pm. Céline paid for them at a website called lastminute. com. We're going to see lots of other shows by getting last-minute tickets.

* * * * * *

I have just discovered charity shops. There are several in Mayford and they sell second-hand things such as clothes, books and furniture. Sometimes they sell beautiful designer clothes, shoes and bags. I was looking in a charity shop today when I found a vintage dress designed by Mary Quant. I tried it on and it fitted me perfectly. It was very cheap so I bought it and I'm really pleased with it!

A new au pair is coming to Mayford next week! She is called Anna and she is from Naples. Her host mother is a friend of my host mum's. The family was planning to get an au pair and decided to invite Anna to stay for a week to see if they could all work well together. So they paid for her plane ticket to England and after a week they all decided it was a good idea. Anna has flown back to Naples to prepare for her stay here and is going to return next week. I'm sure she'll be happy with her new family.

\* \* \* \* \* \* \*

Tonight we are going clubbing in London. There are three of us going - Céline and I plus a Swedish au pair from our English class, Christina. It'll be great fun! We're planning to get the train to London at 9pm and go to a really cool night club near Charing Cross. We're staying out all night and we're coming back in the morning. My host mum wants me to come back to Mayford on the last train from London but I've told her we're going to stay out all night. The first train back to Mayford in the morning leaves London at 5.34am so we're coming back on that train.

Last night was terrible! First of all, on the way to the nightclub, the heel of one of Christina's shoes broke off, so she couldn't walk properly. When we got there, she took her shoes off in order to dance and left them in a corner, but someone stole them so she had no shoes at all!

Céline was chatting to a man at the bar and he bought her a drink. After a few minutes, I saw Céline laughing quite a lot. She looked drunk so I went to see if she was okay. She laughed at me and then started to fall over. I caught hold of her and suddenly she went to sleep in my arms. I think that the man at the bar put something in her drink to make her get drunk.

I wanted to phone my host mum but I lost my phone and I couldn't remember the home phone number. We missed the last train so we spent all our money paying for a taxi back to Céline's house in Mayford. She didn't have her keys, so we had to ring the doorbell. It was 3am. Céline's host mum was shocked. Céline can't remember anything except having a drink at the bar and Christina is really annoyed about her shoes. I am going to buy a new phone. I'm not planning to stay out all night in London again.

# Useful tips

Get a weekly magazine called Time Out to see what's happening in London. It lists free attractions such as museums, parks, street markets and concerts as well as details of shows, musicals, clubs, bars and restaurants in London.

You can get tickets to West End musicals at a reduced price by going to **www.lastminute.com**

Beware of drugs which can be put in your drink while you're not looking at bars and at parties. These drugs make you feel drunk or fall asleep and make you vulnerable to sexual attack.

Memorise your host family's phone number and address so that you can contact them in an emergency even if you have lost your mobile phone.

# Brush up on your English ...

### Future
*'Going to'*
The present continuous of 'to go' can be used to talk about something we intend to do in the future. e.g. She is going to return next week.

*'Planning to'*
'Planning to' is also used to talk about a future intention but shows that we have given it careful thought. e.g. The family was planning to get an au pair.

### Present continuous for future actions
Present continuous can be used to talk about something that we intend to do in the future.
e.g. Tonight we are going clubbing.

### Present simple for future events

Scheduled or regular events which take place in the future use the present simple.

e.g. The first train leaves at 5.34am.

### Will

We use 'will' to predict something in the future or when we expect something to happen in the future.

e.g. It'll (it will) be great fun!

## Have a go!

---

**4A.** Find three examples in the text of 'going to', then put them into negative form.

**1.**

**2.**

**3.**

**4B.** Find three examples in the text of 'planning to'.

**1.**

**2.**

**3.**

**4C.** Find three examples in the text of the present continuous for a future action, then put them into question form.

**1.**

**2.**

**3.**

**4D.** Find one example of 'will' used to predict something in the future, then make it negative.

**1.**

**See p.84 for answers.**

# 5. I love children

This morning I was woken up at 6am by a big, wet kiss. It was Daisy. She came into my room and asked me to play with her. I said, "Daisy, I'm sleeping." She laughed and said, "Silly Marta, you're awake!" and then she started jumping on the bed.

The children's grandmother said, "Children should be seen and not heard." In my experience, the opposite is true. Eliza and Charlie are very loud, but I do not see them very often. They are both busy children with lots of activities such as football, swimming and dance lessons. When they are at home they always argue and shout at each other.

Daisy is very cute. She has a lovely smile but she is also very bossy. She has a miniature teapot with cups and little teaspoons, plates and little plastic cakes. When she plays, she puts all her cuddly toys in a circle on a blanket and she offers them tea and cakes.

Céline takes care of twin girls. Their behaviour is quite challenging. They whisper to each other, they take things from her room and sometimes they say unkind things to her. I am impressed by Céline's reaction. She never gets upset or loses her temper. She has younger twin sisters at home and she says she knows it will take some time for the girls to accept her.

## CHAPTER 5

Last night, at about 9pm, I was walking through Mayford to get some milk from the shops, when I met Olga in the street. She said she was going to get a take-away pizza, so I walked with her to the pizzeria. As we walked past an Indian restaurant, I saw a man and a woman seated near the window looking at us with strange expressions. A moment later, the woman was running after us and shouting angrily. I was shocked! It was Olga's host mother. She was furious because Olga was supposed to be at home babysitting! Later that week Olga was sent back to Lithuania.

\* \* \* \* \* \* \*

This evening, Anna phoned me asking for help. She was babysitting while her host parents were out. They have a two-year-old boy called William who doesn't like being put to bed. Anna said she was frightened by William's behaviour. Then I heard a terrible scream. It sounded like someone was being murdered! Anna was standing at the top of the stairs, holding the phone near William's bedroom door while he was screaming in his cot. She said she couldn't contact the parents on their phones. Anna lives near me, so I walked to her house. When I got there, I was stunned. Anna was singing a beautiful lullaby in Italian and William, almost hypnotised by her voice, was smiling at her!

Christina has three children to look after. The youngest, Toby, is friends with Charlie in my family. Charlie and Toby play together in the holidays. Yesterday, Charlie had a play date at Toby's house. He was very excited about it because he wanted to see his friend again.

We arrived at 2pm. Christina made a pot of tea for us and the boys were sent outside to play in the garden. After a few minutes, Christina looked out of the window and saw Toby standing on the roof of the garden shed. He is not allowed to do this and she was immediately angry with him. She called him into the house and started shouting at him. Toby was rude and imitated Christina's accent. After that, Christina became even more angry so she made him go to his room for the rest of the afternoon. Then, Charlie got upset because his play date was ruined. It was boring for Charlie without his friend, so I asked Christina if Toby could be allowed out of his room to play again. She was surprised by my question and said Toby had to be punished. So I took Charlie home and we played with his Lego. I think perhaps Christina is a little too strict.

# Useful tips

It takes time for you to know the children in your host family and it may take even longer for the children to accept you into the family.

Ask your host parents how they want you to deal with bad behaviour.

Be patient and be consistent - it is best not to lose your temper.

If a child is rude to you try not to be offended; explain to them how they can behave better.

# Brush up on your English ...

### Passive
The passive is formed by using be + past participle.
e.g. Children should be seen and not heard.

We use the passive when we want to talk about an action but we are not interested in who or what does it.
e.g. Olga was sent back to Lithuania.

If you want to say who or what does the action, then use 'by'.
e.g. I was woken up by a big, wet kiss.

Written reports and formal communications often use the passive form.

### Adjectives ending in -ing / -ed
'-ing' adjectives describe the thing or person that has an effect.
e.g. It's exciting (it makes me feel excited).

'-ed' adjectives describe our feelings about something or someone.
e.g. I'm surprised (it surprises me).

# Have a go!

---

**5A.** Choose the correct form of adjective in the sentences below.

**1.** Their behaviour is quite challenged / challenging.

**2.** Charlie is very excited / exciting about his play date.

**3.** It was bored / boring for Charlie without his friend.

**4.** She was surprised / surprising by my question.

**5B.** Use the text to complete these passive sentences with the correct verb form.

**1.** Anna _____ by William's behaviour. (frighten)

**2.** It will take some time for Céline _____ by the twins. (accept)

**3.** The boys _____ outside to play. (send)

**4.** Charlie was upset because his play date _____ . (ruin)

**5C.** Turn these sentences from active to passive form.

**1.** The twins take things from Céline's room.
**2.** Christina made a pot of tea.
**3.** Anna put William to bed.
**4.** Christina sent Toby to his room.

**1.**

**2.**

**3.**

**4.**

**See p.85 for answers**

# 6. I need more money!

My host father has just told me that there is a pub in Mayford which is advertising for a part-time bar assistant to work on Sundays. I am free on Sundays. I think I'll apply. I need to save as much money as possible while I am here so that I can go travelling. I know another au pair who's got a job at a pub and she says it's great fun.

\* \* \* \* \* \* \*

I was sitting in a café yesterday, with Daisy, having a drink and some cake, when I noticed an old lady who was looking at me. She was sitting alone at a table with a pot of tea and a newspaper, but every now and then, she stopped reading her paper and stared at me. Finally, she got up to pay her bill and walked past our table. As she passed me, she pointed at the Mary Quant dress I was wearing, the one I'd bought from the charity shop, and said, "It looks much nicer on you than it ever did on me." She smiled and then walked out of the café. Cool!

Today I received my National Insurance number. This means I can get another job, in addition to working as an au pair. It was quite easy to get it. I went to the local government office called *JobCentre Plus* for an application form which I took home, filled in and sent off. Then they wrote to me and asked me to go for an interview and to take several forms of identity. I took my passport, a letter which I had from the au pair agency, my birth certificate and my driving licence from Poland. A few weeks later, my National Insurance number came in the post. Now I can do some extra work and earn some more money.

\* \* \* \* \* \* \*

Today was Daisy's birthday. She is now four years old. She loves the presents that her family gave her. We had a birthday party for Daisy and invited some children who go to her nursery. Eliza and Charlie were very helpful with the party games. First there was *Musical Statues*, in which the children must stay very still whenever the music stops. Then, in *Pin The Tail On The Donkey*, we put a blindfold on a child who had to try and remember where to put the donkey's tail on a picture.

We also played *Pass The Parcel*. This is a game in which the children hand round a parcel in a big circle and whenever the music stops the child who's got the parcel can take off one layer of wrapping paper. Unfortunately, there was a fight when one child, whose behaviour was very aggressive, attacked another child to get the parcel! There was lots of screaming and crying, but in the end Eliza distracted them both with a balloon and the game continued.

After the party games, the children ate a birthday tea we had made - little cheese sandwiches, sausage rolls and a trifle made with sponge, custard, jelly and cream. Finally, Daisy's mummy brought out a beautiful birthday cake with four candles that Daisy blew out as we all sang "Happy Birthday!" At bedtime, Daisy gave me a big hug and said it was the best birthday ever!

* * * * * * *

Yesterday Céline invited me to go with her to visit her French friend, Sylvie, who works as an au pair for a family about 12 miles from here. We went on the M25 motorway which is 117 miles long and is one of the biggest orbital roads in Europe. Céline estimated the journey to be no more than 30 minutes, but it took two hours and 30 minutes! We accidentally went the wrong way around the M25, driving over 100 miles to get there. Next time I will check the map before we set off!

I am now a bar maid! The pub is really cool. I have to arrive at 10am and make sure all the glasses are clean and ready. I must also check that the tables and chairs are clean and ready. It is my job to collect the dirty glasses and wash them in the glass washer and help with serving food from the kitchen. I really like the people I've met. There are two bar maids whose jobs are to serve the drinks at the bar and the bar man who is also the pub landlord. In the kitchen there are two chefs whose responsibilities are the roast lunches and the puddings.

\* \* \* \* \* \* \*

My host mum has advised me to open a bank account so I can keep my money safe. She asked the bank where she keeps her money what documents are needed for me to open an account. The man at the bank said that I need my passport and a letter from the au pair agency addressed to the manager of the bank to confirm that I am here as an au pair. The letter must also confirm all my personal details such as my date of birth, how long I will stay here and how much my family pays me.

# Useful tips

If you want to get extra work you must first obtain a National Insurance number. This enables you to work and pay tax in the UK.
See **www.gov.uk** for details of how to apply.

To open a bank account in the UK you must have your passport and a letter on headed paper from the au pair agency addressed to the bank, stating your full name, date of birth, your host family's address, your length of contract and your salary.

# Brush up on your English ...

## Relative clauses

A clause is a part of a sentence. A relative clause is used to give more information about people or things by using a relative pronoun.

### Who / That / Which
'Who' and 'that' are used to refer to people.
'Which' and 'that' are used to refer to things.
e.g. I know an au pair who's (who has) got a job at a pub.
e.g. There is a pub in Mayford which is advertising for a bar assistant.

'Who is' and 'who has' can both be shortened to who's. Do not confuse this with 'whose' (see below).

'Who' / 'that' / 'which' can be omitted if they refer to people or things which are the object of the verb in the relative clause.
e.g. Daisy loves the presents (which / that) her family gave her.

### Whose
'Whose' is used in relative clauses instead of 'his' / 'her' / 'their'.
e.g. There is a child whose behaviour is very aggressive.

**Where**

'Where' is used in a relative clause to talk about a place.

e.g. She asked the bank where she keeps her money.

## Have a go!

---

**6A.** Use the text to put in the correct relative pronoun - 'who' / 'that' / 'which' / 'whose'.

**1.** I know an au pair ＿＿＿＿＿＿ has got another job in a pub.

**2.** I took a letter ＿＿＿＿＿＿ I had from the au pair agency.

**3.** The children ate the birthday tea ＿＿＿＿＿＿ we made.

**4.** We invited some children ＿＿＿＿＿＿ go to Daisy's nursery.

**5.** I put a blindfold on a child ＿＿＿＿＿＿ had to remember where to put the donkey's tail.

**6.** The cake had four candles ＿＿＿＿＿＿ Daisy blew out.

**7.** The child ＿＿＿＿＿＿ has got the parcel.

**8.** The people ＿＿＿＿＿＿ I've met.

**9.** A barman ＿＿＿＿＿＿ is also the pub landlord.

**10.** Two chefs ＿＿＿＿＿＿ responsibilities are the roast lunches and the puddings.

**6B.** Which of the sentences above can omit the relative pronoun?

**6C.** Rewrite these sentences using a relative pronoun.

**1.** There is a pub in Mayford. It is advertising for a bar assistant.
**2.** There are two barmaids. Their jobs are to serve drinks.
**3.** I have a national insurance number. I need it if I want to get a job.
**4.** I keep my money in a bank. It is safe.
**5.** Daisy's birthday is today. She is four years old.

**Answers**

**1.**

**2.**

**3.**

**4.**

**5.**

**See p.85 for answers.**

# 7. Get me a doctor ... and a midwife too!

My finger hurts. There is a little cut under my ring which is very sore and my finger is swollen. Sometimes I'm in quite a lot of pain. I have shown it to my host mum and she wants me to see a doctor. I can walk to the doctor's surgery in Mayford so I'll go there this morning to register as a patient and then I can make an appointment.

\* \* \* \* \* \* \*

They didn't have any appointments available this morning so I had to wait until this afternoon to see the doctor. I have an infection in my finger and I must take some antibiotics. The doctor gave me a prescription so I went to the pharmacy in Mayford and collected my medicine. The prescription cost less money than I expected. I have quite a lot of pills and I must take one every day until they are all finished.

\* \* \* \* \* \* \*

Christina saved the life of her family's dog! Toby was playing cricket in the garden and accidentally hit the dog in the chest with a cricket bat. The dog stopped breathing but Christina gave it the kiss of life and resuscitated it. Now Toby thinks she is the best au pair in the world!

## CHAPTER 7

I have finished the course of antibiotics and now there is no pain or swelling in my finger so I think the infection has cleared up. But poor Anna has sent me a text to say she has chickenpox! She caught it from William. I can see her photo on Facebook and she has lots of red spots all over her face. William has fewer spots than Anna but he has had a fever too. They both have to stay at home until

they are no longer contagious. My host mum doesn't want to catch any infections as she is eight months pregnant, so we are keeping away from Anna's family for the time being.

* * * * * * *

It's a boy! I am feeling very proud of myself! My host father has given me lots of flowers and has said thank you so many times. It was an

incredible experience ... I came into the kitchen at about midnight to get some water. I saw my host mum, in her dressing gown, leaning against the table. She suddenly swore loudly and shouted, "There isn't much time!" I felt frightened. She knelt down on the floor and told me to look in her bag for the number of the midwife at the hospital.

I realised that the baby must be coming early, called the hospital and waited a few moments for someone to answer. My host mum was holding the back of a chair and was in a lot of pain. Luckily the children were all asleep in bed, but unluckily, my host father was away in Paris!

The midwife who answered the phone said, "How many minutes are there between each contraction?" Just at that moment, loads of water suddenly spilled all over the kitchen floor! I asked my host mum, "How many minutes are there between each contraction?" but she only shouted, "There's no bloody time!" The midwife on the phone said, "Can you see anything coming?" and I said, "Yes, it's moving forwards and backwards!" I dropped the phone, grabbed a cushion and put it underneath my host mum, just as the baby came out.

"Thank Heavens for that! Oh, it's a little boy!" said my host mum. Then I wrapped the baby in some clean tea towels, gave him to my host mum and picked up the phone again. The baby's crying was so loud that I could hardly hear the midwife, but several minutes later, an ambulance arrived. There was so much mess to clear up afterwards!

# Useful tips

Free healthcare is available on the National Health Service. It is advisable to register with your nearest doctor's surgery when you arrive so that you can make an appointment as soon as you have any health problems.

Most adults must pay a prescription charge for their medicine.

Emergency contraception treatment is available free of charge from the doctor's surgery, from some pharmacies or from contraceptive clinics if you present within 72 hours of having unprotected sex.
See **www.fpa.org.uk** for further details of sexual health advice and treatment.

First aid courses which cover emergency life support procedures in adults, children and infants are available at St John Ambulance.
See **www.sja.org.uk** for further details.

# Brush up on your English ...

### Countable & uncountable nouns
Countable nouns can have a singular and a plural form.
e.g. minute (singular)
        minutes (plural)
Uncountable nouns do not have a plural form.
e.g. time

### Much/Many
'Much' is used with uncountable nouns.
e.g. There isn't much time
'Many' is used with countable nouns.
e.g. How many minutes?

## Quantifiers with countable nouns

many / so many / too many / a few / fewer / several / one or two / a couple of

## Quantifiers with uncountable nouns

much / so much / too much / a bit of / less / a little

## Quantifiers with both countable and uncountable nouns

some / a lot of / lots of / loads of / any / enough / no

## Have a go!

**7A.** Choose the correct quantifier in each sentence.

**1.** My finger is giving me any / a lot of / several pain.

**2.** There were no / much / a little appointments at the doctor's surgery this morning.

**3.** The doctor has prescribed a little / so much / some antibiotics.

**4.** William has enough / fewer / some spots than Anna.

**5.** My host mum doesn't want to catch so much / some / any infections.

**6.** My host father gave me lots of / a bit of / any flowers.

**7.** I came into the kitchen to get several / some / a couple of water.

**8.** There isn't many / much / some time!

**9.** I found some / a bit of / much clean tea towels.

**10.** There was a lot of / loads of / so much mess.

**See p.86 for answers.**

# 8. Home cooking

My host mum is incredibly busy with the new baby, Archie, so she has asked if I could do the cooking for the next two or three weeks. I'm not a very good cook, but I'm willing to try!

Yesterday, I made my favourite dish from Poland - beetroot soup with mushroom dumplings. I went shopping in the morning especially to buy the beetroot, cabbage and mushrooms that I needed and then I spent all afternoon cooking.

The children came home from school and I served up my special Polish meal. They hated it, even Daisy who normally likes beetroot. Charlie refused to try it and Eliza said the smell of my dumplings made her feel sick. I was so disappointed that I wanted to cry, but I said I would make cheese on toast for them instead.

Today I tried to cook something simple. My host mum told me there were some bags of scampi in the freezer, so I decided to cook them in the oven and serve them with potatoes, broccoli and peas.

Disaster! The instructions on the packet said I had to cook the scampi in the oven for 15 minutes at 220 degrees. The oven temperature was only 120 degrees and the scampi were not cooked properly. Charlie said they were disgusting and Eliza said, "Marta, you're not a very good cook." Daisy, who had been hungry before, said she wasn't hungry any more.

* * * * * * *

We have eaten Shepherd's Pie three times this week and I can't stand it any more! My host mum said I should just make pasta because it is easy but instead I cooked sausages with mashed potatoes, steamed carrot and buttered cabbage. The children loved it and Eliza said I was 'quite' a good cook!

I was very pleased with myself until I realised I had done something really stupid. I had poured the fat from the sausages down the sink and completely blocked the drain. My host dad had to disconnect the pipes under the sink and clean out the fat. I said I was very sorry. He said it was okay, as long as I didn't do it again.

Next week, Anna is coming to stay with us for a week. Her host mother is going away on holiday to stay with relatives. She is taking her child with her but she can't take Anna. So Anna asked whether she could stay with a friend instead of being at home with the host father, and she is going to sleep on a camp bed in my room. Cool!

\* \* \* \* \* \* \*

I have put on weight and now my clothes don't fit! The problem is that I am not eating enough salad or fresh fruit and I snack too often on the children's biscuits, cakes and yoghurt which are always in the kitchen. I don't get much exercise, either. I will ask whether I can join a gym so that I can get into better shape.

\* \* \* \* \* \* \*

Céline is a good cook. She has shown me some of the things that she makes for her host family. She said her children didn't like eating vegetables so she had to disguise them in soups and casseroles. She has given me a wonderful recipe for a beef casserole which she cooks very slowly in the oven. She also makes some delicious soups which she blends and serves with croutons. Céline said I should read my host mum's cookery books for ideas.

Today my host mum asked me how well I knew Ricardo. I said that I knew him quite well because I saw him each week at English classes. Then she asked if I ever noticed what kind of clothes he wore. I thought about it and said that sometimes he wore smart shirts and jackets and once he came to school in a very stylish sheepskin coat! My host mum smiled knowingly. Then she told me that Ricardo was in the habit of borrowing his host father's clothes without permission! We both laughed but really I felt quite shocked by his behaviour. His host parents have warned him not to do it any more.

* * * * * * *

Going to the gym makes me feel much better! I asked if I could join as a temporary member so it is not too expensive and now I can swim and use the exercise machines every day if I want to. Why didn't I think of this before?

# Useful tips

Use your host family's cookery books to find meals that everyone will like.

Look for a gym that offers membership at a reduced rate.

See page 96 for some easy and delicious recipes.

# Brush up on your English ...

### Indirect speech

We use indirect speech when we don't want to repeat the actual words that were said.

e.g. "There are some bags of scampi in the freezer," she said.
   She said there were some bags of scampi in the freezer.

You can use 'that' to connect the first verb with the indirect speech, or you can omit it.

e.g. She said (that) there were some bags of scampi in the freezer.

In indirect speech, the verb usually changes to the nearest past tense.

e.g. He said "It's okay, as long as you don't do it again."
   He said it was okay as long as I didn't do it again.

| Direct speech | | Indirect speech |
|---|---|---|
| We eat | - | we ate |
| We are eating | - | we were eating |
| We have eaten | - | we had eaten |
| We ate | - | we had eaten |
| We are going to eat | - | we were going to eat |
| He will eat | - | we would eat |
| He can eat | - | we could eat |

**would / could / should / ought / might**

If these verbs are used in direct speech, they do not change in indirect speech.

e.g. "Could you do the cooking for the next few weeks?" she asked.

She asked if I could do the cooking for the next few weeks.

"You should use your host mum's cookery books," said Céline.

Céline said I should use my host mum's cookery books.

**Indirect questions**

Ask is followed by 'if' or 'whether'.

e.g. She asked if I could cook for the next few weeks.

## Have a go!

**8A.** Change these sentences from direct speech to indirect speech.

**1.** "Marta, could you do the cooking for the next few weeks?" she asked.

**2.** "I'm going shopping to buy some beetroot, cabbage and mushrooms," she said.

**3.** He said, "The smell of those dumplings makes me feel sick!"

**4.** "I'm not hungry any more," replied Daisy.

**5.** I shouted, "I can't stand Shepherd's Pie any more!"

**6.** "You should just make pasta because it's easy," said my host mum.

**7.** "I realise I've done something really stupid," I said.

**8.** Daisy said, "You're quite a good cook."

**9.** "I will ask if I can join a gym," she said.

**10.** "Can I join as a temporary member?" she asked.

**Answers**

**1.**

**2.**

**3.**

**4.**

**5.**

**6.**

**7.**

**8.**

**9.**

**10.**

**8B.** Change these sentences from indirect speech to direct speech.

**1.** My host mum said she was incredibly busy with the new baby.
**2.** Marta said she had spent all afternoon cooking.
**3.** The children said the food was disgusting.
**4.** I said I would make cheese on toast.
**5.** Marta said she had put on weight.
**6.** Céline told me her children didn't like eating vegetables.
**7.** She said I should read some cookery books.
**8.** Marta said the problem was she snacked too often on biscuits and cake.
**9.** Marta asked whether she could join a gym.
**10.** She said she felt much better.

**Answers**

**1.**

**2.**

**3.**

**4.**

**5.**

**6.**

**7.**

**8.**

**9.**

**10.**

**See p.87 for answers.**

# 9. Free time and travel

If it's a bank holiday, it rains! We have had three bank holiday weekends recently and each of them has been rainy. Apparently, this is typically English weather!

\* \* \* \* \* \* \*

Christina has gone back to Sweden for a holiday. She left yesterday and her host mother is annoyed about it. Christina said it was Walpurgis Night. If you're from Sweden, you celebrate Walpurgis Night with a bonfire party and everyone has a holiday the next day. Christina wanted to go back to celebrate with her family and friends. Her host family did not know about it until the day before she left, but Christina said she told them months ago. Sometimes people need to communicate more!

\* \* \* \* \* \* \*

Next month my host family is going on holiday. They are driving to France and will spend two weeks there. My host mum has asked me to stay at home and look after the cat while they are away.

She told me I could invite my family to stay here with me. Cool! If my host family is away, I'll be free to visit lots of places with my parents. And if my parents hire a car then we will be able to drive everywhere!

\* \* \* \* \* \* \*

I have discovered English Heritage and the National Trust. They are organisations that restore historic buildings. They own some amazing old castles and houses that have beautiful gardens and they are perfect for day trips. If my parents get a special visitors' pass we will be able to able to visit these wonderful places together.

\* \* \* \* \* \* \*

Yesterday in my English class we did a practice exam paper for the Cambridge First Certificate. It was very difficult. If I pass my exam I will be able to get a better job in Poland, so I really want to do well. My teacher always says that you make more progress if you study little and often, so I am dedicating an hour each day to studying English grammar and vocabulary.

My parents arrived today from Poland and tomorrow my host family sets off on holiday. My parents don't speak much English so I have to translate everything for them. We had a lovely dinner together with my host family. My host mum cooked a leg of lamb which we had with roast parsnips, roast potatoes, spinach, asparagus and a delicious gravy. My parents think the children are beautiful! Tomorrow we are going to visit Cambridge and if the weather is nice we will hire a boat and take a trip down the river.

\* \* \* \* \* \* \*

Cambridge was wonderful but there was one problem. We thought it looked easy to use the boat on the river, but actually it was

quite difficult. The boats are called punts and you have to drop a long pole into the water and push off the bottom of the river bed to make the punt move. My dad had a go and he was quite good at it. Then I had a go, but the pole got stuck in the mud and I couldn't pull it out again. The boat moved forward, I stayed with the pole, then I slid down into the water! I was drenched from head to toe!

\* \* \* \* \* \* \*

We are having a lovely holiday here. The weather is fantastic! Today we went

to London to visit Greenwich. We went on a river boat from The Embankment all the way down the Thames. At Greenwich, we had a picnic in the park and visited The Royal Observatory Museum which is really cool because it's located on the Greenwich Meridian dividing the East from the West.

It was very crowded on the way home and we got separated from my mother in the London Underground. The doors of the tube closed before she could get off, so I shouted through the glass window, "If you get off at the next stop and wait, we will meet you there!" Luckily, another train came a minute later and we found my mum at the next stop.

# Useful tips

Agree with your host family how much holiday you can have and make sure you agree the dates in advance.

Ask English Heritage **www.english-heritage.org.uk** and the National Trust **www.nationaltrust.org.uk** about their junior rates and overseas visitors passes. These will allow you to visit their stately homes, castles and gardens.

For a list of interesting places to visit see appendices 2 & 3.

You can find some lovely nature walks in the countryside in your local area if you go to **www.wildlifetrusts.org**.

# Brush up on your English ...

## Conditional

### General Conditional
The general conditional is used to state a general rule, a pattern of behaviour or a logical conclusion.
e.g. If you're from Sweden, you celebrate Walpurgis Night.

It can also be used for ironic effect
e.g. If it's a bank holiday weekend, it rains!

### First Conditional
The first conditional is used to talk about a strong possibility in the future. It consists of a present or future verb in the 'if' clause and a future verb in the main clause.
e.g. If my parents hire a car, we will be able to drive everywhere.

The 'if' clause can come before or after the other clause. There is a comma after the 'if' clause if it is at the start of the sentence.

e.g. We will be able to drive everywhere if my parents hire a car.

     If my parents hire a car, we will be able to drive everywhere.

## Have a go!

**9A.** Find three examples of a general conditional sentence in the text above.

**1.**

**2.**

**3.**

**9B.** Put the verbs into the correct form for the first conditional.

**1.** If my parents come to England, I _____ lots of places with them. (visit)

**2.** If they _____ , I will translate for them. (not / understand)

**3.** It will be easy to get a good job if I _____ my First Certificate in English. (pass)

**4.** If the weather _____ nice, we will hire a boat. (be)

**5.** I _____ the cat if you go on holiday. (look after)

**9C.** Put these conditional sentences into question form.

**1.** If it's a bank holiday, it rains.
**2.** We will hire a boat if the weather's nice.
**3.** If you're from Sweden, you celebrate Walpurgis Night.
**4.** We will visit Greenwich if we have enough time.
**5.** If we go to France, we will go by car.

**Answers**

1.

2.

3.

4.

5.

See p.87 for answers

# 10. I need to pass these exams

Next week we're taking our First Certificate exam. We have done quite a few practice papers and my scores are getting pretty good. Last night my host father was trying to help me with a paper but he had to give up because some of the grammar questions were

too difficult for him! He said, "Sorry, Marta, if I knew the answer to that question, I'd tell you, but it's too tricky."

I have been keeping a notebook ever since I first arrived so that I can write down new words and expressions. It's been extremely useful because I find the words easy to remember when I write them down.

Céline, Anna, Christina and I have all been working together to practise for the speaking test. On the day of the exam, we have to speak with a partner so I have chosen to speak with Céline and Anna will speak with Christina. If I were bilingual, this exam would be easy!

\* \* \* \* \* \* \*

Céline's friend, Sylvie, the one who lives with a host family 12 miles around the M25, came to visit us in Mayford today. She has asked

Céline to help her find a new family in Mayford because she's not happy with her present family. According to Sylvie, this is because her host family tries to restrict her social life. According to Céline, Sylvie is always inviting her friends from France to visit for the weekend and she expects her host family to accomodate them all! If I were Céline, I wouldn't introduce Sylvie to any families looking for an au pair.

\* \* \* \* \* \* \*

Today we had our speaking test. I overslept! I only had 10 minutes to get dressed and get to the train station. Céline was waiting to meet me at the station and we went on the 8am train. We thought it would be a simple journey, but in fact, it was really stressful. The exam centre was very hard to find and we got lost. If we had known, we would have planned our journey better. We arrived five minutes late, but luckily the examiner was running late too!

\* \* \* \* \* \* \*

Today, Christina, Céline, Ricardo and I went to Anna's house for the afternoon. Anna's host parents both work during the day and the little boy, William, goes to a nursery. As we've all been studying

hard, we decided to have some fun! Anna set up the karaoke player and Ricardo started off with a very good impression of Michael Jackson. We soon got into ABBA and the afternoon just disappeared because we were having such a good time. Just as we were all singing and dancing to the chorus of *Money, money, money*, there was a loud knock on the window. It was the next-door neighbour, complaining that the music was too loud and threatening to call the police! Anna went to apologise and we all went home to do some more revision. Tomorrow we have the rest of our exam papers. I wouldn't have overslept if I had gone to bed earlier last time, so tonight I am going to bed at 9pm!

\* \* \* \* \* \* \*

Thank goodness that's over! I think the exam went okay. Ricardo had a terrible time. He had kept his mobile phone in his pocket and the alarm went off during the exam. The invigilator said Ricardo could be disqualified for cheating. The rules say you must not take mobile phones into the exam room. If he'd remembered his phone was in his pocket, he'd have left it with the people at reception. Now he might be have to retake the exam.

# Useful tips

Get some past exam papers and start trying them about three months before your exam.

Find out where the exam will take place and rehearse your journey there to minimise any stress on the day of your exam.

Make sure you read the regulations about what you can and can't take into the exam room.

# Brush up on your English ...

## Conditional

### Second conditional

The second conditional is used when we are talking about a hypothetical situation in the present or future.

It is formed by using 'if' plus the past simple or past continuous, with 'would' in the main clause.
e.g. If I knew the answer to that question, I would tell you.

However, you should use 'were' instead of 'was', when using the first person singular.
e.g. If I were bilingual, this exam would be easy.

### Third conditional

Third conditional is used when we are talking about a hypothetical situation in the past. It is formed by using 'if' plus past perfect, with 'would have' in the main clause.
e.g. If I had gone to bed earlier, I wouldn't have overslept.

# Have a go!

**10A.** Put the verb into the correct form.

**1.** If you got distinction in your exam, you _____ be thrilled. (be)

**2.** If we _____ any later, we would have missed our speaking test. (arrive)

**3.** If I _____ you, I would plan your journey to the exam centre. (be)

**4.** If Ricardo got disqualified he _____ the exam. (retake)

**5.** If my host father _____ help me with my grammar, he would. (can)

**6.** I would have been better prepared if I _____ more revision. (do)

**7.** If I had gone to bed earlier, I _____ . (not oversleep)

**10B.** Put the main clause in the sentences below into negative form.

**1.** If he knew the answer, he would tell me.
**2.** If they had missed the train, they would have been late.
**3.** If I had more time, I would do more revision.
**4.** You would have got distinction if you had studied more

**Answers**

**1.**

**2.**

**3.**

**4.**

**10C.** Put the sentences above into question form.

**Answers**

1.

2.

3.

4.

**10D.** Put the sentences above into negative question form.

**Answers**

1.

2.

3.

4.

**See p.88 for answers.**

# 11. I love my phone

**To:** Céline
**From:** Marta
R U going 2 pub 2nite?
CU there 8pm?

**To:** Marta
**From:** Céline
OK CU l8er X

**To:** Céline
**From:** Marta
@ pub. Where R U?

**To:** Marta
**From:** Céline
IMS! Have to BaBsit!

**To:** Céline
**From:** Marta
OK! BFN. X

**To:** Marta
**From:** 47789765800
RU free @ wknd?
Harry

**To:** 47789765800
**From:** Marta
DIKU?

**To:** Marta
**From:** 47789765800
We met @ pub.
R U free 4 a drink?

**To:** 47789765800
**From:** Marta
Maybe

**To:** Marta
**From:** 47790765800
Gr8. CU Sat 8pm @
same pub?

**To:** 47789765800
**From:** Marta
CWL

**To:** Céline
**From:** Marta
OMG Got a d8!

**To:** Marta
**From:** Céline
Wow!
FF X

* * * * * * *

**To:** Céline
**From:** Marta
WYWH

**To:** Marta
**From:** Céline
RU OK?

**To:** Céline
**From:** Marta
With d8. ZZZ

**To:** Marta
**From:** Céline
LOL

**To:** Marta
**From:** Harry
Dinner 2nite?

**To:** Marta
**From:** Harry
Hot4U!

**To:** Marta
**From:** Harry
CW2CU. XOXO

**To:** Marta
**From:** Harry
ILUVU

\* \* \* \* \* \* \*

**To:** Marta
**From:** Céline
How's Yr BF?

**To:** Céline
**From:** Marta
PITA

**To:** Marta
**From:** Céline
WAN2TLK?

**To:** Harry
**From:** Marta
Harry needs 2 GAL ASAP.
Got SOHF & MSGs R OTT.
Will tell him 2 TAH.

**To:** Marta
**From:** Harry
OIC. NRN

**To:** Céline
**From:** Marta
AAAAGHH!
Sent yr msg 2 Harry!

**To:** Céline
**From:** Marta
ROFL C U 2moro
X

# Useful tips

Get a UK phone so that you do not have to pay expensive overseas tariffs on your own phone.

Make a note of your phone's 15-digit IMEI (International Mobile Equipment Identity) number, usually printed under the battery. If your phone is stolen, tell your service provider so they can block the phone's usage.

Never respond to emails or texts asking for your bank details as these are scams to obtain your money.

Psychological research shows that people feel happier when they switch off their phones and enjoy face-to-face conversation with friends and family.

# Brush up on your English ...

## Texting

| | | |
|---|---|---|
| **2nite** | - | tonight |
| **2moro** | - | tomorrow |
| **4** | - | for |
| **@** | - | at |
| **ASAP** | - | as soon as possible |
| **BaBsit** | - | babysit |
| **BF** | - | boyfriend |
| **BFN** | - | bye for now |
| **CU** | - | see you |
| **CWL** | - | cool |
| **D8** | - | date |
| **DIKU** | - | do I know you? |
| **FF** | - | friends forever |

| | | |
|---|---|---|
| **GAL** | - | get a life |
| **ILUVU** | - | I love you |
| **IMS** | - | I am sorry |
| **L8er** | - | later |
| **LOL** | - | laughing out loud |
| **MSG** | - | message |
| **NRN** | - | no reply needed |
| **OIC** | - | oh I see! |
| **OMG!** | - | oh my God! |
| **OTT** | - | over the top |
| **PITA** | - | pain in the arse |
| **RU** | - | are you |
| **ROFL** | - | rolling on the floor laughing |
| **SOHF** | - | sense of humour failure |
| **TAH** | - | take a hike |
| **Wan2talk?** | - | do you want to talk? |
| **Wknd** | - | weekend |
| **WYWH** | - | wish you were here |
| **X** | - | kiss |
| **XOXO** | - | hugs and kisses |
| **Yr** | - | your |
| **ZZZ** | - | boring |

# 12. Sweet sorrow

All good things come to an end, don't they? My host parents have asked me if I would like to stay for another year, but I have saved quite a bit of money and have decided to travel across Europe with Céline and Christina before returning to Poland. There's such a lot to see in Europe, isn't there?

My host mum has been very helpful and has helped us to plan our journey. We have decided to buy an InterRail pass which is very good value for people under 26. We are going to take a few sleeper trains but most of our overnight accommodation will be in hostels. We each have a big rucksack and while we are visiting various cities we will leave our rucksacks in station lockers so that we don't have to carry our luggage around.

## CHAPTER 12

My host mum keeps asking me, "You will keep in touch, won't you?" and my host dad has asked me, "You won't be going off with any strange men, will you?" But we're all sensible and nobody's going to come to any harm, are they? I mean, nothing's going to go wrong, is it?

* * * * * * *

Here we are at the station. My host mum says, "You've got your tickets, haven't you?" Eliza asks me, "You're coming back to visit, aren't you, Marta?" I have promised to come back again and visit next year.

Now I suddenly feel very upset. Charlie says, "You're sad, aren't you? You don't have to go back to Poland, do you?" I'm hugging them tightly. Daisy says, "We've got time for a special cuddle before the train comes, haven't we?" I am nearly crying. She gives me one of her big, wet kisses and says, "You liked being with us, didn't you, Marta?"

I'm on the train with Céline and Christina. We all agree, that was a great year, wasn't it?

# Useful tips

To get an InterRail Pass go to **www.raileurope.co.uk**
It is best to plan your itinerary and book your accommodation in advance.

Use a bank card to access your money from cash machines.

Give your itinerary to relatives so they know where you are.

# Brush up on your English ...

### Questions tags

In questions which use the present or past simple, the question tag is formed with 'do' or 'did'.
e.g. All good things come to an end, don't they?
    You liked it here, didn't you?

In questions which contain 'be' and 'have', the same verb is also used in the question tag.
e.g. You're sad, aren't you?
    You've got your tickets, haven't you?

In questions that have more than one auxiliary, the question tag is formed using the first auxiliary verb.
e.g. You won't be going off with any strange men, will you?
    You don't have to go back to Poland, do you?

Questions containing modal verbs (can, will, should) use the same modal verb in the tag.
eg. You will keep in touch, won't you?

Tag questions can also be made with 'there'
e.g. There's such a lot to see in Europe, isn't there?

Some negative words such as 'nothing' or nobody' can also be used with question tags.

e.g. Nothing's going to go wrong, is it?

Nobody's going to come to any harm, are they?

Question tags usually require a 'yes' or 'no' answer.

e.g. You won't be going off with any strange men, will you?

No, I won't.

You will keep in touch, won't you?

Yes, I will.

That was a great year, wasn't it?

Yes, it was!

## Have a go!

**12A.** Add a tag to complete these questions.

**1.** InterRailing is great fun, _____?

**2.** You like travelling, _____?

**3.** We spent a year in England, _____?

**4.** They shouldn't take too much luggage, _____?

**5.** They will need rucksacks, _____?

**6.** I can go anywhere in Europe, _____?

**7.** Nobody wants you to go, _____?

**8.** There are so many places to visit in Europe _____?

**9.** You can come back again, _____?

**10.** We will miss you, _____?

**See p.89 for answers.**

## 1A

| | ✓ |
|---|---|
| **1.** have | ⬚ |
| **2.** do you wake up | ⬚ |
| **3.** works | ⬚ |
| **4.** doesn't smell | ⬚ |
| **5.** do you like | ⬚ |
| **6.** I am doing | ⬚ |
| **7.** doesn't understand | ⬚ |
| **8.** I am still ironing | ⬚ |
| **9.** go | ⬚ |
| **10.** know | ⬚ |

## 2A

| | ✓ |
|---|---|
| • asked Eliza | ⬚ |
| • cried Daisy | ⬚ |
| • yelled Charlie | ⬚ |
| • shouted my new host mother | ⬚ |
| • they called | ⬚ |
| • I changed | ⬚ |
| • my host mum asked | ⬚ |
| • I went | ⬚ |
| • my host mum suddenly asked | ⬚ |
| • I didn't understand | ⬚ |
| • I just smiled | ⬚ |
| • my host mum laughed | ⬚ |
| • my host mum took | ⬚ |
| • Eliza said | ⬚ |
| • Mr Fisher exploded | ⬚ |
| • I was surprised | ⬚ |
| • I went | ⬚ |

- it was easy      ◯
- I gave           ◯
- I met            ◯

**2B**

- I was working with my first family.   ◯
- Last night I was reading in my room.  ◯
- I was enjoying the programme.         ◯

**2C**

- I have already changed families.      ◯
- I have just learnt a new expression.  ◯
- I have just received an email.        ◯
- She has now separated from her husband. ◯
- I have started my English classes.    ◯
- She has given us some homework.        ◯

**2D**

- I have been staying in the UK for less than a week. ◯
- I have been spending a lot of time.   ◯
- She has been suffering a lot of stress. ◯
- We have been working together all evening. ◯

---

**3A**                                  ✓

**1.** must / have to      ◯
**2.** can                 ◯
**3.** can't / mustn't     ◯
**4.** mustn't             ◯
**5.** don't have to       ◯
**6.** has to / must       ◯
**7.** can                 ◯
**8.** must                ◯

**9.** can't ○

**10.** have to ○

---

**4A**

- I'm going to try and see a musical / I'm not going to try and see a  musical. ✓

- We're going to see lots of other shows / We're not going to see lots of other shows. ○

- We're going to stay out all night / We're not going to stay out all night. ○

- Anna is going to return next week / Anna is not going to return next week. ○

- I'm going to buy a new phone / I'm not going to buy a new phone. ○

**4B**

- I am planning to do more exciting things. ○
- The family was planning to get an au pair. ○
- We are planning to get the train at 9pm. ○
- I'm not planning to stay out all night in London again! ○

**4C**

- A new au pair is coming to Mayford / Is a new au pair coming to Mayford? ○

- Tonight we are going clubbing in London / Are we going clubbing in London tonight? ○

- We're staying out all night / Are we staying out all night? ○

- We're coming back in the morning / Are we coming back in the morning? ○

- We're coming back on that train / Are we coming back on that train? ○

**4D**

- I'm sure she'll be happy / I'm sure she won't be happy. ⭕
- It'll be great fun / It won't be great fun. ⭕

---

**5A** ✔

1. challenging ⭕
2. excited ⭕
3. boring ⭕
4. surprised ⭕

**5B**

1. was frightened ⭕
2. to be accepted ⭕
3. were sent ⭕
4. was ruined ⭕

**5C**

1. Things are taken from Céline's room by the twins. ⭕
2. A pot of tea was made by Christina. ⭕
3. William was put to bed by Anna. ⭕
4. Toby was sent to his room by Christina. ⭕

---

**6A** ✔

1. who ⭕
2. that / which ⭕
3. that / which ⭕
4. who ⭕
5. who ⭕
6. which / that ⭕

**7.** who       ○

**8.** who / that    ○

**9.** who       ○

**10.** whose     ○

## 6B

- I took a letter I had been given by the au pair agency.    ○
- The children ate the birthday tea we made.    ○
- The cake had four candles Daisy blew out.    ○
- The people I've met.    ○

## 6C

- There is a pub in Mayford which is advertising for a bar assistant.    ○
- There are two barmaids whose jobs are to serve drinks.    ○
- I have a National Insurance number which I need if I want to get a job.    ○
- I keep my money in a bank where it is safe.    ○
- Daisy, whose birthday is today, is four years old.    ○

## 7A       ✓

**1.** a lot of    ○

**2.** no    ○

**3.** some    ○

**4.** fewer    ○

**5.** any    ○

**6.** lots of    ○

**7.** some    ○

**8.** much    ○

**9.** some    ○

**10.** All three are correct.    ○

## 8A

1. She asked Marta if she could do the cooking for the next few weeks. ✓
2. She said she was going shopping to buy some beetroot, cabbage and mushrooms. ○
3. He said the smell of the dumpling made him feel sick. ○
4. Daisy replied that she wasn't hungry any more. ○
5. I shouted that I couldn't stand Shepherd's Pie any more. ○
6. My host mum said I should just make pasta because it was easy. ○
7. I said I realised I had done something really stupid. ○
8. Daisy said that I was quite a good cook. ○
9. She said she would ask if she could join a gym. ○
10. She asked if she could join as a temporary member. ○

## 8B

1. "I'm incredibly busy with the new baby," said my host mum. ○
2. "I have spent all afternoon cooking," said Marta. ○
3. "The food is disgusting!" said the children. ○
4. "I will make cheese on toast," I said. ○
5. "I've put on weight," said Marta. ○
6. "My children don't like eating vegetables," said Céline. ○
7. "You should read some cookery books," she said. ○
8. "The problem is I snack too often on biscuits and cake," said Marta. ○
9. "Can I join a gym?" asked Marta. ○
10. "I feel much better," she said. ○

---

## 9A

1. If it's a bank holiday, it rains. ✓ ○
2. If you're from Sweden, you celebrate Walpurgis Night. ○
3. You make more progress if you study little and often. ○

**9B**

1. will visit ⭕
2. don't understand ⭕
3. pass ⭕
4. is ⭕
5. will look after ⭕

**9C**

1. If it's a bank holiday, does it rain? ⭕
2. Will we hire a boat if the weather's nice? ⭕
3. If you're from Sweden, do you celebrate Walpurgis Night? ⭕
4. Will we visit Greenwich if we have enough time? ⭕
5. If we go to France, will we go by car? ⭕

---

**10A** ✓

1. would be ⭕
2. had arrived ⭕
3. were ⭕
4. would retake ⭕
5. could ⭕
6. had done ⭕
7. would not have overslept ⭕

**10B**

1. If he knew the answer, he wouldn't tell me. ⭕
2. If they had missed the train, they wouldn't have been late. ⭕
3. If I had more time, I wouldn't do more revision. ⭕
4. I wouldn't have got distinction if I had studied more. ⭕

**10C**

1. If he knew the answer, would he tell me? ⭕

**2.** If they had missed the train, would they have been late?   ○

**3.** If I had more time, would I do more revision?   ○

**4.** Would you have got distinction if you had studied more?   ○

## 10D

**1.** If he knew the answer, wouldn't he tell me?   ○

**2.** If they had missed the train, wouldn't they have been late?   ○

**3.** If I had more time, wouldn't I do more revision?   ○

**4.** Wouldn't you have got distinction if you had studied more?   ○

---

## 12A

✓

**1.** isn't it?   ○

**2.** don't you?   ○

**3.** didn't we?   ○

**4.** should they?   ○

**5.** won't they?   ○

**6.** can't I?   ○

**7.** do they?   ○

**8.** aren't there?   ○

**9.** can't you?   ○

**10.** won't we?   ○

# Free-entry London attractions

## Street Markets

| | |
|---|---|
| Borough Market | www.boroughmarket.org.uk |
| Brick Lane | www.visitbricklane.org |
| Camden Passage | www.camdenlock.net |
| Columbia Road | www.columbiaroad.info |
| Portobello Road | www.portobelloroad.co.uk |

## Museums

| | |
|---|---|
| The British Museum | www.britishmuseum.org |
| The Victoria & Albert Museum | www.vam.ac.uk |
| The Natural History Museum | www.nhm.ac.uk |
| The Science Museum | www.sciencemuseum.org.uk |

## Art Galleries

| | |
|---|---|
| The National Gallery | www.nationalgallery.org.uk |
| The National Portrait Gallery | www.npg.org.uk |
| Tate Britain | www.tate.org.uk |
| Tate Modern | www.tate.org.uk |
| Serpentine Gallery | www.serpentinegallery.org |
| The Wallace Collection | www.wallacecollection.org |

## Parks

www.royalparks.org.uk

Regent's Park and Primrose Hill  /  Green Park  /  Hyde Park
St James's Park  /  Kensington Gardens  /  Brompton Cemetery
Richmond Park  /  Bushey Park  /  Greenwich Park

# Day trips near London

**Arundel, Kent**
Distance:                              63 miles southwest of London
London train station:                                         Victoria

Things to see & do:                   Arundel Castle and Gardens
                                                    Cathedral
                                              Wetland Centre
                                      Boat trip on River Arun

**Brighton, Sussex**

| | |
|---|---|
| Distance: | 54 miles south of London |
| London train station: | Victoria |

Things to see & do:

Royal Pavilion
Brighton Pier
The Lanes
Pebble beach
Brighton Museum and Art Gallery

**Cambridge, East Anglia**

Distance: 60 miles northeast of London

London train station: King's Cross or Liverpool Street
By coach with National Express: From Victoria Coach Station

Things to see and & do:

Punting on River Cam
Botanic Gardens
Fitzwilliam Museum
Kettle's Yard Art Gallery
Parker's Piece and Midsummer Common

**Canterbury, Kent**
Distance:                                          63 miles southeast of London
London train station:                          Victoria or Charing Cross
By coach with National Express:     From Victoria Coach Station

Things to see & do:                              Canterbury Cathedral
                                                            Roman Museum
                                              Norman castle and gardens
                                               Boat trip on River Stour


**Colchester, Essex**
Distance:                                          60 miles northeast of London
London train station:                                    Liverpool Street

Things to see & do:                               Colchester Museum
                                                            Castle Park
                                                            Boating lake
                                                   Firstsite Art Gallery


**Lewes, East Sussex**
Distance:                                          57 miles south of London
London train station:                                              Victoria

Things to see & do:                                       Lewes Castle
                                              Anne of Cleves's House
                                                            Priory Park
                         Bonfire Night celebrations on 5 November

**Newbury, Berkshire**

| | |
|---|---|
| Distance: | 60 miles west of London |
| London train station: | Paddington |

Things to see & do:

Newbury Racecourse
Shaw House Museum
Donnington Castle
Highclere Castle
Boat trip on Kennet & Avon Canal

**Oxford, Oxfordshire**

| | |
|---|---|
| Distance: | 60 miles west of London |
| London train station: | Paddington |
| By Coach with Oxford Tube: | See website for bus stops |
| or National Express: | Victoria Coach Station |

Things to see & do:

Ashmolean Museum
Cherwell Boat House
Punting on River Cherwell
University Parks
Botanic Gardens
Christ Church Picture Gallery

**Windsor, Berkshire**
Distance:                              25 miles west of London
London train station:                          Paddington

Things to see & do:                        Windsor Castle
Changing of the Guard
Windsor Great Park
Boat trip on Thames River
Eton College
Ascot Racecourse


**Whitstable, Kent**
Distance:                              62 miles east of London
By train:                             Victoria or St Pancras

Things to see & do:                              Beach
Harbour
Whitstable Museum & Gallery
Alley Ways
Whitstable Castle
Oyster bars

# Easy recipes

## Shepherd's Pie
Serves 6 with leftovers

### Ingredients
1k minced lamb meat
1 large onion
1 large carrot
2 sticks celery
1 clove garlic
a little red or white wine (optional)
800g tinned whole tomatoes
a teaspoon of dried basil or thyme
1k potatoes
25g butter
25g grated cheese (optional)

### Method

**1.** Finely chop the onion, carrot and celery.

**2.** Heat 2 tablespoons of mild olive oil in a large saucepan, add the chopped vegetables and cook gently until they are softened.

**3.** Add the minced lamb and mix in with the vegetables for a few minutes.

**4.** Add the wine, crushed garlic, herbs, salt and pepper and cook for a few more minutes.

**5.** Add the tinned tomatoes and stir gently, without breaking up the tomatoes. Simmer gently for about 40 minutes, stirring occasionally.

**6.** Meanwhile, peel and wash the potatoes and cut into quarters. Place in a large pan with cold water, bring to the boil and cook until they are soft.

**7.** Drain and mash the potatoes with the butter and season with salt and pepper.

**8.** Now break up the tomatoes in the meat mixture, check the seasoning and place in a baking dish about 5cm deep. Spread the mashed potatoes on top and sprinkle with grated cheese.

**9.** Bake in a pre-heated oven at 180 degrees for about 40 minutes.

**10.** Serve with vegetables or salad.

## Baked potato and salad

**Ingredients**
1 medium or large potato per person
Mild olive oil
Salt

Toppings can include:
butter, mayonnaise, grated cheese, tinned tuna fish, tinned mackerel or heated baked beans

## Method

**1.** Heat the oven to 180 degrees.

**2.** Wash the potatoes, remove any blemishes and dry thoroughly. Prick each potato with a fork. Rub a little olive oil over the potato skins and sprinkle with a little salt.

**3.** Bake in the oven for about an hour (depending on size) until the skins are crispy and they are soft and fluffy inside. Serve with a topping of your choice and salad.

## Tuna and tomato pasta sauce
Serves 6

**Ingredients**
680g tomato passata
200g tinned tuna fish
1 or 2 cloves of garlic
Mild olive oil

## Method

**1.** Gently heat 3 tablespoons of mild olive oil in a heavy-bottomed pan, add the passata and slowly bring to the boil.

**2.** Add the tuna fish, the crushed garlic and some salt and pepper. Gently simmer for about 40 minutes, stirring occasionally.

**3.** Serve with cooked linguine or pasta shapes such as penne, rigatoni, farfalle or fusilli.

## Lentil soup
Serves 6

### Ingredients
1 large onion
1 large carrot
3 sticks of celery
3 tablespoons mild olive oil
1 litre vegetable or chicken stock
1 litre boiling water
120g red split lentils
Juice of a lemon

### Method

**1.** Roughly chop the onion, carrot and celery.

**2.** Heat 3 tablespoons of mild olive oil in a large saucepan and gently cook the chopped onion, carrot and celery for about 10 or 15 minutes until softened.

**3.** Meanwhile place lentils in a large bowl, wash and rinse several times under a running tap, using a sieve, until thoroughly cleaned.

**4.** Pour the hot stock and boiling water over the vegetables. Add the lentils, bring to the boil and simmer for 40 minutes, stirring occasionally.

**5.** Blend the mixture and transfer to a clean pan. Season with salt and pepper according to taste and add lemon juice.

**6.** Serve with crusty bread and cheese.

# Fish in breadcrumbs

Serves 6

## Ingredients

6 fillets of fresh white fish
(e.g. lemon sole, plaice, haddock,
cod, coley or whiting with skins removed
- ask the fishmonger to do this for you.)
2 or 3 large eggs
2 or 3 tablespoons flour
6 tablespoons breadcrumbs
30g parmesan cheese
4 tablespoons mild olive oil

## Method

**1.** Place flour in a wide shallow bowl and mix in a little salt and pepper. Beat the eggs in another bowl.

**2.** Grate the parmesan cheese and mix with the breadcrumbs in a third shallow bowl.

**3.** Coat each piece of fish in the flour, then the egg and finally the breadcrumb mixture.

**4.** Put the coated fish on a large dish and leave in the fridge until you are ready to cook them.

**5.** When you are ready to eat, heat the mild olive oil in a large non-stick frying pan and gently fry the coated fish for 2 minutes on each side until golden-brown.

**6.** Transfer the fish to a dish in an oven heated to about 150 degrees to keep warm until every piece is cooked. Serve with mashed potato or chips and peas.

## Cheese on toast

**Ingredients**
1 or 2 slices of bread per person
25g grated cheese per person

**Method**

**1.** Heat the grill.

**2.** Lightly toast the bread in the toaster. Place grated cheese on the toast.

**3.** Cook under the grill until the cheese just starts to bubble. Serve with salad.

## Sardines on toast

**Ingredients**
1 or 2 slices of bread per person
Butter
Tinned sardines (children
prefer boneless sardines)
Lemon

**Method**

**1.** Toast the bread in the toaster and spread a little butter on each slice.

**2.** Place sardines on the toast and flatten down with a knife.

**3.** Squeeze a little lemon juice over the top.

**4.** Serve with salad.

## Scrambled eggs on toast

**Ingredients**
1 or 2 eggs per person
1 or 2 slices of bread per person
Butter

**Method**

**1.** Toast the bread in the toaster and spread a little butter on each slice.

**2.** Beat the eggs in a bowl and season with salt and pepper.

**3.** Melt a knob of butter in a non-stick frying pan, add the eggs and stir with wooden spoon until the eggs start to solidify.

**4.** Place the scrambled eggs on the slices of toast and serve immediately.

## Beef Casserole
Serves 6

### Ingredients
1.2 kilos stewing beef,
cut into 3cm squares
4 medium-sized onions
500ml bottle of pale ale
2 tablespoons flour
4 tablespoons mild olive oil
2 teaspoons thyme
1 bay leaf
2 cloves garlic
3 tablespoons Geo Watkins Mushroom Ketchup
(available at supermarkets)

### Method

**1.** Heat the oven to 125 degrees.

**2.** Trim the fat off the meat and cut into 3cm cubes.

**3.** Peel and roughly chop the onions.

**4.** Heat the oil in a large casserole dish and cook the meat on a high heat until browned.

**5.** Remove the meat from the pan using a slotted spoon and put aside.

**6.** Add the chopped onion to the pan and cook in the remaining oil and meat juices on a high heat for five minutes, until softened.

**7.** Return the meat to the pan, turn down the heat, add the flour and stir with a wooden spoon until the flour has soaked up all the meat juices.

**8.** Slowly pour in the pale ale and gently bring to simmering point.

**9.** Add thyme, bay, garlic and mushroom ketchup and stir gently.

**10.** When it starts to simmer, place lid on the casserole and put in the oven to cook for 3 hours.

**11.** Check seasoning and serve with rice or mashed potatoes and vegetables.

## Victoria Sponge Cake

**Ingredients**
110g self-raising flour
1 tsp baking powder
110g soft butter
110g caster sugar
2 large eggs
1 tsp vanilla essence
2 tablespoons jam for the filling
A little icing sugar to dust on top

**Method**

**1.** Heat the oven to 170 degrees.

**2.** Prepare two 18cm-cake tins by greasing them with a little butter and lining the bottoms with baking parchment.

**3.** Using a sieve, sift the flour and baking powder into a large mixing bowl.

**4.** Add all the rest of the ingredients and mix with an electric mixer.

**5.** Pour half the mixture into each cake tin and spread it out to the sides of the tin.

**6.** Bake in the middle of the oven for 30 minutes till golden brown.

**7.** Turn out of the cake tins and let them cool on a wire rack.

**8.** Remove the baking parchment, spread the jam on one half and sandwich together.

**9.** Dust the top with a little icing sugar. Serve with a cup of tea.

## Apple Crumble
Serves 6

**Ingredients**
6 apples (800g)
Juice of half a lemon
100g maple syrup
150g rolled oats
1tsp cinnamon
100g ground almonds (optional)
100g soft brown sugar
100g cold butter

## Method

**1.** Heat the oven to 175 degrees.

**2.** Peel the apples and cut into quarters, remove the cores, and slice finely.

**3.** Mix the apples in a bowl with the maple syrup and lemon juice.

**4.** Place apple mixture in a buttered baking dish.

**5.** In another bowl, mix the oats, cinnamon, ground almonds and sugar.

**6.** Cut the butter into small pieces and rub into the oat mixture until crumbly.

**7.** Pour the crumble mixture on top of the apples.

**8.** Bake for 40 minutes until brown on top and bubbling at the sides.

**9.** Serve for pudding with cream or vanilla ice-cream.

## Gingerbread

### Ingredients
225g self-raising flour
1.5 teaspoons ground ginger
Half a teaspoon mixed spice
100g soft brown sugar
100g butter

100g golden syrup
100g treacle
1 large egg
150ml milk

**Method**

**1.** Heat oven to 175 degrees.

**2.** Grease a square (22cm) baking tin and line with baking parchment.

**3.** Put sugar, butter, syrup and treacle in a pan and gently heat till melted.

**4.** Put the flour and spices into a mixing bowl.

**5.** Gradually add the treacle mixture to the flour and mix with an electric mixer.

**6.** Beat the egg and milk together, then gradually mix into the flour and treacle mixture.

**7.** Pour into the baking tin and bake for 30 minutes.

**8.** Serve with a cup of tea, or as a pudding with vanilla ice cream.

# Index